EVERYDAY MYSTERIES

HOW DO ROCKS FORM?

By John O'Mara

Gareth Stevens
PUBLISHING

Please visit our website, www.garethstevens.com. For a free color catalog of all our high-quality books, call toll free 1-800-542-2595 or fax 1-877-542-2596.

Cataloging-in-Publication Data

Names: O'Mara, John.
Title: How do rocks form? / John O'Mara.
Description: New York : Gareth Stevens Publishing, 2021. | Series: Everyday mysteries | Includes glossary and index.
Identifiers: ISBN 9781538256596 (pbk.) | ISBN 9781538256619 (library bound) | ISBN 9781538256602 (6 pack)
Subjects: LCSH: Rocks–Juvenile literature. | Geology–Juvenile literature.
Classification: LCC QE432.2 O43 2021 | DDC 552–dc23

Published in 2021 by
Gareth Stevens Publishing
111 East 14th Street, Suite 349
New York, NY 10003

Editor: Therese Shea

Photo credits: Cover, p. 1 Ralf Lehmann/Shutterstock.com; pp. 3–24 (background) Natutik/Shutterstock.com; p. 5 alexreynolds/Shutterstock.com; p. 7 Lukasz Kochanek/Shutterstock.com; p. 9 Thijs Peters/Shutterstock.com; p. 11 LesPalenik/Shutterstock.com; p. 13 Heather Lucia Snow/Shutterstock.com; p. 15 Walter Bilotta/Shutterstock.com; p. 17 Barna Tanko/Shutterstock.com; p. 19 Albert Russ/Shutterstock.com; p. 21 Nasky/Shutterstock.com.

Printed in the United States of America

CPSIA compliance information: Batch #CS20GS: For further information contact Gareth Stevens, New York, New York at 1-800-542-2595.

CONTENTS

Boldface words appear in the glossary.

Let's Rock!

Rocks are everywhere you look. They're in our roads, on our beaches, and a part of our gardens. They're in places you can't see too. They're under the grass and deep under the ground. Did you ever wonder how rocks form?

Our Rocky Earth

The outer layer of Earth is mostly rock. What is a rock? It's matter that is made up of one or more **minerals** that have been joined together. Different **processes** of nature cause different kinds of rocks to form.

Rocks are all sizes. Some are so large that people climb them. Other rocks are tiny. Bits of sand are rocks! Not all rocks are hard. Magma is molten, or melted, rock within Earth. When it comes to the **surface**, it's called lava.

lava

Name Those Rocks

There are three main kinds of rocks. Igneous rocks form from magma. Magma may become hard under the ground. It also may come out of a **volcano** and cool on Earth's surface. Granite is a kind of igneous rock.

granite

Sedimentary rock forms when **weathering** and **erosion** break rocks apart. Rock pieces called sediment gather in rivers, oceans, deserts, and other places. Sediment builds up and compacts, or is forced together. It becomes solid rock. Sandstone is a kind of sedimentary rock.

sandstone

Metamorphic rock comes from igneous or sedimentary rock that has been changed by heat or **pressure** inside Earth. Metamorphic rock also forms when water breaks down minerals in igneous or sedimentary rock. Water can add minerals to rock too. Marble is a metamorphic rock.

marble

A Long, Long Process

Igneous, sedimentary, and metamorphic rocks are always breaking down and reforming into new kinds of rocks. This is called the rock cycle. A cycle is a process that happens again and again. The rock cycle takes **millions** of years!

Really Important Rocks

Many kinds of rocks are important to people. Strong rocks are used for building. Some rocks have minerals, **metals**, and gems inside them. We get salt from rocks too! People mine deep within Earth to reach rocks called ores. Ores have minerals and metals in them.

copper ore

Be a Geologist!

When we learn about rocks, we're learning about how Earth works. The study of rocks and how they form and change is called geology. Do you want to be a geologist? You could discover the secrets of Earth's past!

THE ROCK CYCLE

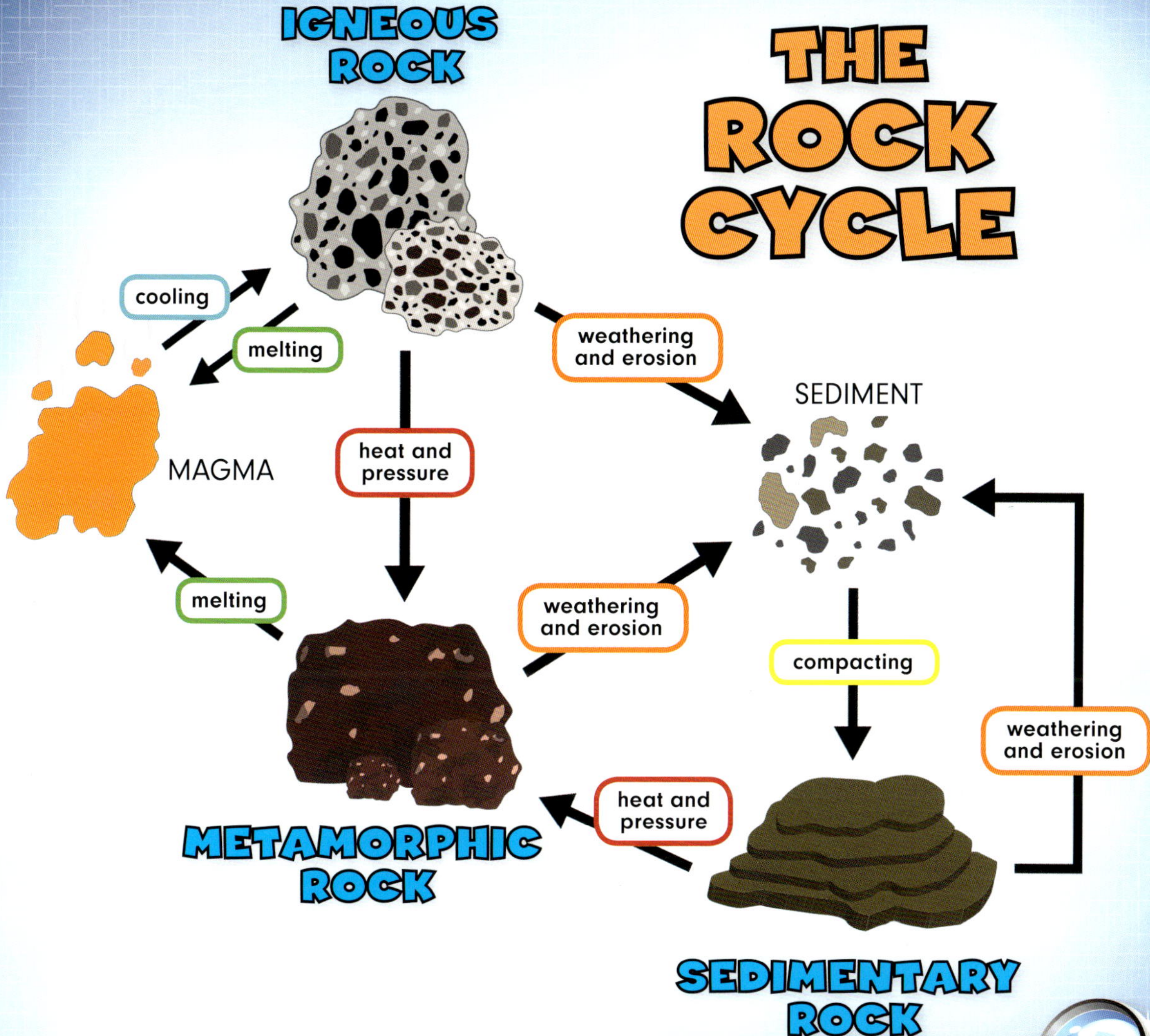

GLOSSARY

erosion: the act of wearing away by water, wind, or ice

metal: a hard, shiny matter found in the ground, such as iron or copper

million: a thousand thousands, or 1,000,000

mineral: matter in the ground that forms rocks

pressure: a force that pushes on something else

process: a series of steps or actions taken to complete something

surface: the top layer of a planet

volcano: an opening in a planet's surface through which hot, liquid rock sometimes flows

weathering: changing in appearance or form by weather such as rain or wind

FOR MORE INFORMATION

BOOKS

Bowman, Chris. *Rocks*. Minneapolis, MN: Bellwether Media, 2015.

Ostopowich, Melanie. *Rocks*. New York, NY: AV2 by Weigl, 2016.

Pettiford, Rebecca. *The Rock Cycle*. Minneapolis, MN: Pogo, 2019.

WEBSITES

Rock Cycle
www.dkfindout.com/us/earth/rock-cycle/
Check out this diagram of the rock cycle.

Rocks and the Rock Cycle
www.ducksters.com/science/rocks.php
Read more about Earth's interesting rocks.

Publisher's note to educators and parents: Our editors have carefully reviewed these websites to ensure that they are suitable for students. Many websites change frequently, however, and we cannot guarantee that a site's future contents will continue to meet our high standards of quality and educational value. Be advised that students should be closely supervised whenever they access the Internet.

INDEX